Workbook

BACKPACK Starter

Second Edition

Mario Herrera · Diane Pinkley

Contributing Writer

Sarah Bupp

PEARSON
Longman

Backpack Starter, Second Edition
Workbook

Pearson Education, 10 Bank Street, White Plains, NY 10606, USA

Staff credits: The people who made up the *Backpack Starter* Workbook team,
representing editorial, production, design, and manufacturing, are Rhea Banker,
Carol Brown, Sarah Bupp, Tracey Cataldo, Gina DiLillo, Christine Edmonds,
Ed Lamprich, Christopher Leonowicz, Maria Pia Marrella, Linda Moser, Leslie Patterson,
Diane Pinkley, Edie Pullman, Robert Ruvo, Susan Saslow, Loretta Steeves, and
Andrew Vaccaro.
Text composition: TSI Graphics
Text font: 16 pt HSP Helvetica Text
Illustrations: Basaluzzo, Constanza, 50; Borlasca, Hector, 80; Briseno, Luis, 1, 5, 49, 51,
60, 70, 71, 81, 83, 93, 94, 95, 99, 100, 101, 102, 103, 106, 108; Catanese, Donna,
49, 51, 63; Ho, Jannie, 65; Kaminski, Karol, 21; 25, 30, Lascaro, Rita, 8, 18, 28, 38, 48,
55, 58, 65, 68, 74, 78, 80, 88, 90; Linstromberg, Ruth, 14, 24, 70, 81; Palmisciano,
Diane, 59, 60; Silver-Thompson, Pattie, 9, 20, 29, 44, 64, 83; Tagel, Peggy, 90; Tobin,
Nancy, 41, 53, 54, 84, 89

ISBN-13: 978-0-13-208483-3
ISBN-10: 0-13-208483-X

PEARSON LONGMAN ON THE **WEB**

Pearsonlongman.com offers online
resources for teachers and students. Access
our Companion Websites, our online catalog,
and our local offices around the world.

Visit us at **pearsonlongman.com**.

Printed in the United States of America
6 7 8 9 10—VO39—13 12 11

Contents

1 Fun in Class

1 Listen and color.

2 Color and cut. Sing and show.

Glue

Students color each picture red or yellow and cut out the pictures. As students sing the song, they hold up the yellow pictures for verse one and the red pictures for verse two.

Listen and color. Color the circles.

4 Count. Circle and say. Listen and check.

⑤ Color and cut. Glue on page 7. ✂

6 Glue. Listen and play Bingo.

7 Listen and chant. Draw a line.

A   b

B   c

C   a

8 Trace. Write.

A a   A   a

B b   B   b

C c   C   c

9 **Read *One, Two, Three.* Draw a line. Say.**

1   **2**   **3**

10 **Do you like the story? Draw a face.**

Review

(11) Listen and circle.

1.

2.

3.

4.

5.

2 My Family

TRACK 9

1 Listen and sing. Cut and glue. Say. ✂

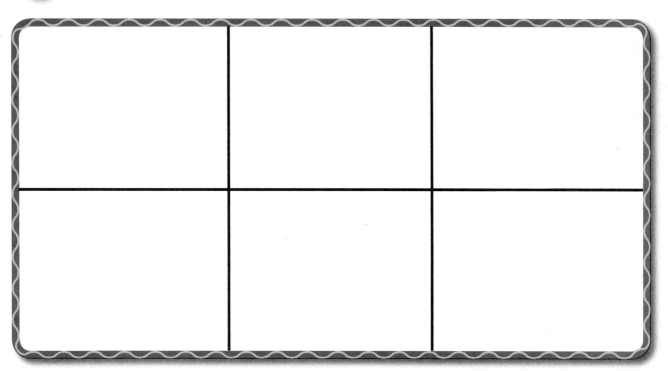

✂ - ✂

Students listen to and sing the song. They cut out the pictures of family members and glue them above. Then they name each person.

2 Draw a room in your house. Who do you see?

3 Count and circle. Listen and check.

4 Trace. Write.

5 **Cut and say. Glue on page 17.** ✂

⑥ Choose and glue. Say.

Students choose where to glue the cards they cut out from page 15. After they glue the cards, have them present their work. For example: *The father is in the living room.*

7 Listen and chant. Draw a line and color.

8 Trace. Write.

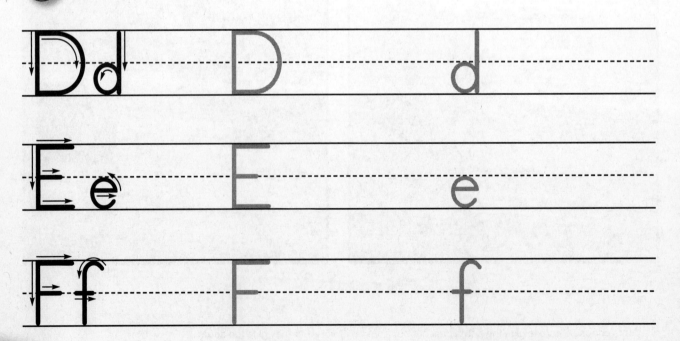

9 **Read *A Mouse Family*. What's missing?**
Draw and say.

10 **Do you like the story? Draw a face.**

   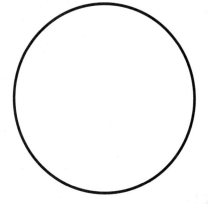

Review

 11 **Listen and circle.**

1.

2.

3.

4.

5.

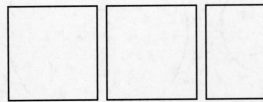 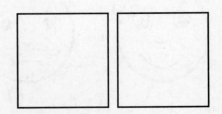

All About Me

 TRACK 13

1 **Cut. Listen and sing. Play.** ✂

Students cut out the pictures of body parts. As they listen to and sing the song, they touch each card to their own body.

2 Trace and color. Point to the triangles.

TRACK 14
3 Listen and color.

 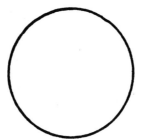 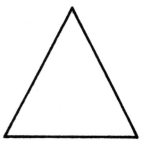

4 **Color and say.**

5 **Look at the robot. Count and circle.**

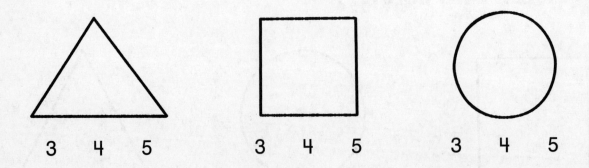

3 4 5   3 4 5   3 4 5

6 Cut and say. Glue on page 27. ✂

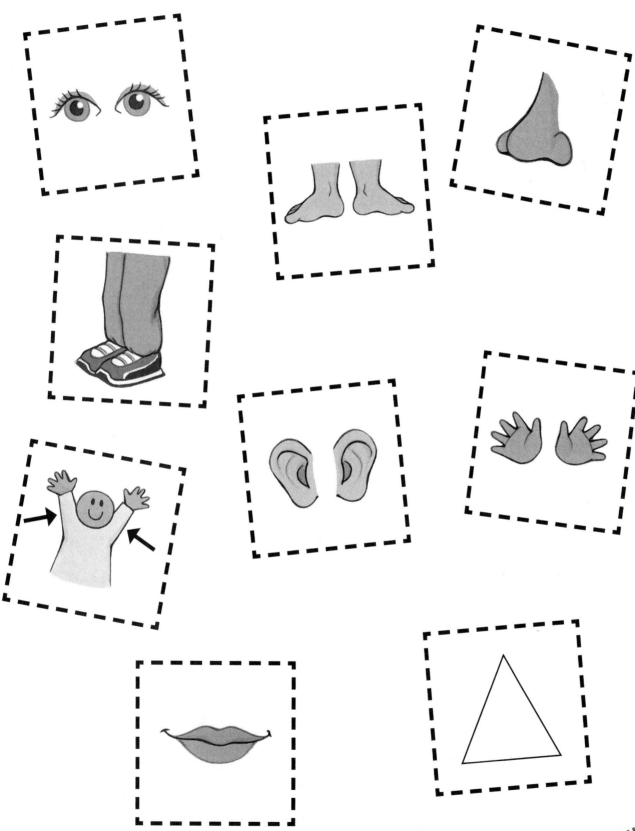

⑦ Glue. Play a game.

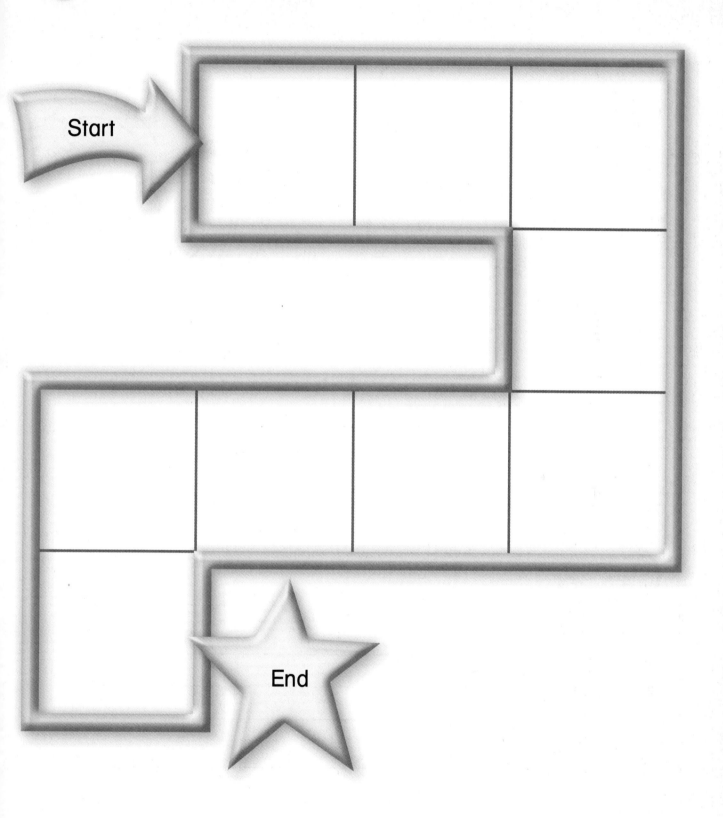

Start

End

Before playing the game, students glue the cards they cut out from page 25 in any order onto the game board. In pairs or small groups, players move one space at a time. If they can name the picture they land on, they stay on that spot. If not, they go back one space.

TRACK 15

8 Listen and chant. Draw a line.

G   h

H   i

I   g

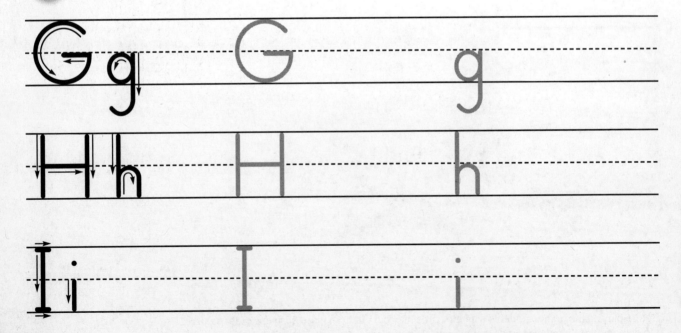

9 Trace. Write.

G g   G   g

H h   H   h

I i   I   i

28

10 **Read *Hide and Seek*. Color.**
Find and count. Say.

11 **Do you like the story? Draw a face.**

Review

12 Listen and circle.

1.

 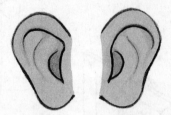

2.

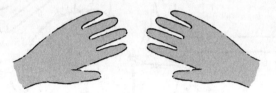 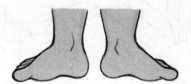

3.

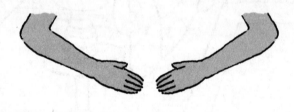 

4.

5.

My Clothes

 1 TRACK 17 **Cut. Listen and sing. Glue.**

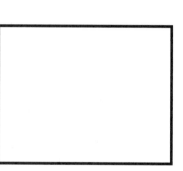

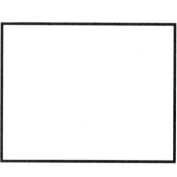

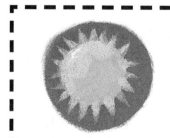

Students cut out the pictures. They listen to and sing the song and glue the appropriate cutout next to each picture.

2 Trace. Color to match.

3 Listen and color.

4 Listen and color. Count and say.

5 Color purple, orange, and blue.
Cut and say. Glue on page 37. ✂

6 Sort and glue. Say.

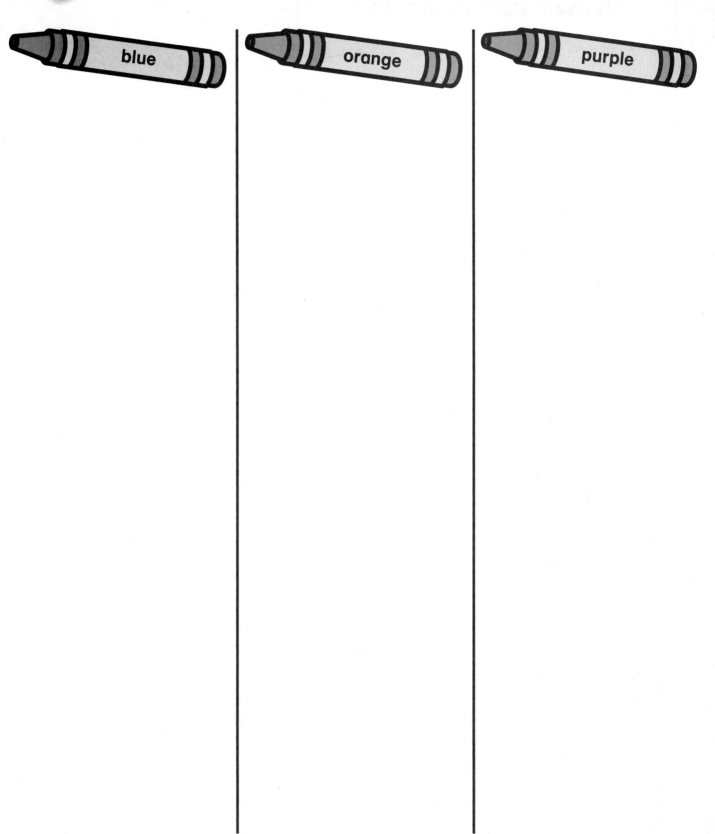

blue

orange

purple

Students sort the cutouts from page 35 by gluing them in the correct columns according to their color. Then they present their work. For example: *It's a jacket. It's blue.* or *It's a blue jacket.*

7 **Listen and chant.**
Draw a line and color.

I j K k L l J

8 **Trace. Write.**

J j   J   j

K k   K   k

L l   L   l

9 **Read *My Shoes*.**
Where are my shoes?
Draw. Point and say.

10 **Do you like the story? Draw a face.**

   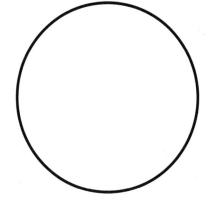

Review

 Listen and circle.

1.

2.

3.

4.

5.

40

At the Toy Store

 1 **Listen and sing. Cut and glue.**

Students listen to and sing the song. They cut out the pictures of the toys and glue them on the correct shelves above.

CHESS GAME

② Listen and color.

③ Trace. Write.

5 ___   6 ___   7 ___

Count and circle. Listen and check.

4   5   6   7

4   5   6   7

4   5   6   7

4   5   6   7

5 Connect the dots from 1 to 7. Color.

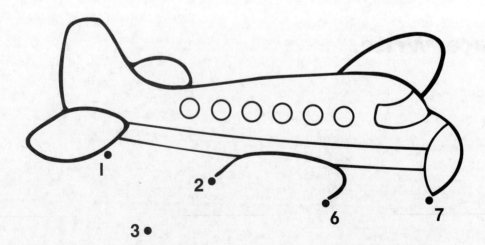

6 **Cut and say. Choose three.**
   Glue on page 47. ✄

7 **Glue three cutouts. Draw and say.**

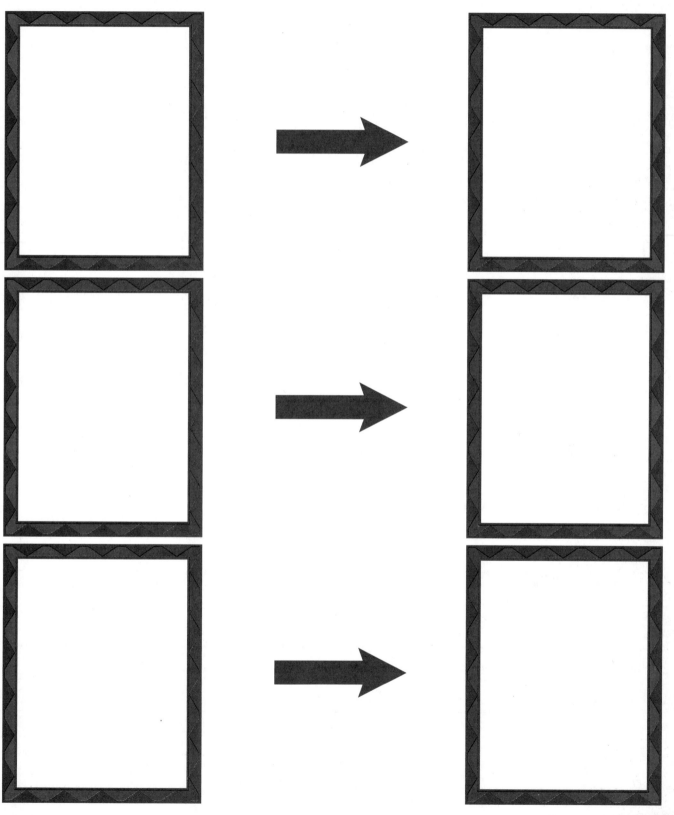

**8 Listen and chant.
Draw a line and color.**

9 Trace. Write.

M m   M   m

N n   N   n

O o   O   o

10 Read *Let's Count*. Count. Write.

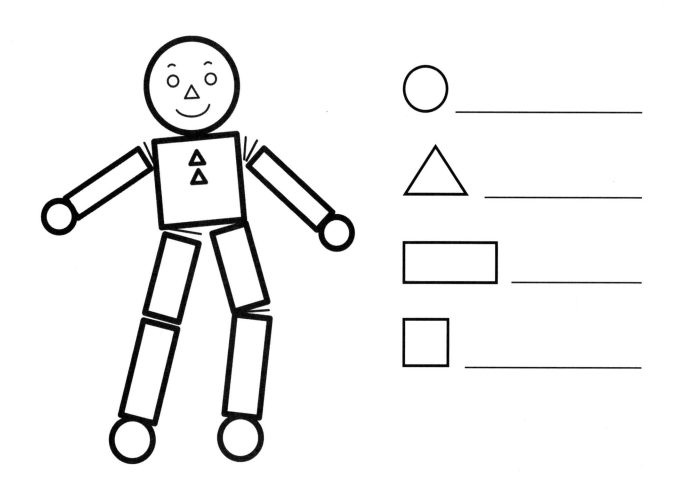

11 Do you like the story? Draw a face.

   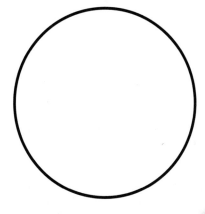

Unit 5

49

Review

 Listen and circle.

1.

2.

3.

4.

5.

People Around Town

TRACK 27

1 Listen and sing. Color.

 -

2 Color and cut. Glue and say.

Students color and cut out the pictures. Then they glue the cutouts to the picture above and name each person.

③ Count and circle.

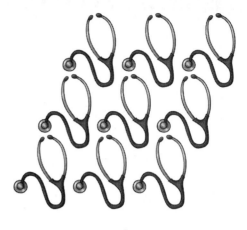

7   8   9   7   8   9

7   8   9   7   8   9

④ Trace. Write.

8   8 _____   8 _____

9   9 _____   9 _____

Listen and count. Trace and write.

6 Count and say. Draw what's missing.

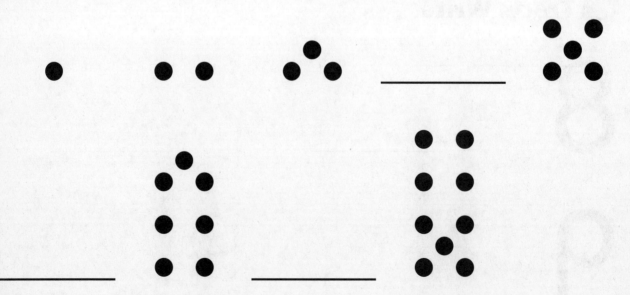

7 Listen and point. Cut and say.
Match and glue on page 57. ✂

8 Match and glue.

9 Listen and chant. Draw a line.

P

Q

R

r

p

q

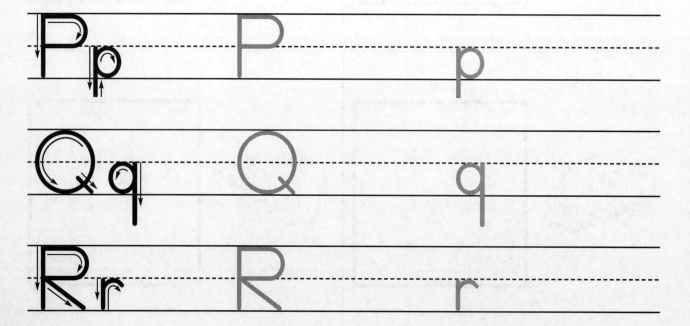

10 Trace. Write.

Pp   P   p

Qq   Q   q

Rr   R   r

11 **Read *The Shopping Trip*.**
Draw a line. Say.

12 **Do you like the story? Draw a face.**

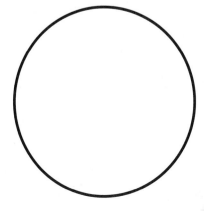

Review

13 **Listen and circle.**

1.

2.

3.

4.

5.

Swinging and Sliding

7

TRACK 32

1 **Listen and sing. Point.**

 2 **Cut. Match and glue.** ✄

Students cut out the action cards and glue them below the matching actions at the top of the page.

3 Listen and write.

TRACK 33

4 **Count. Write and say.**

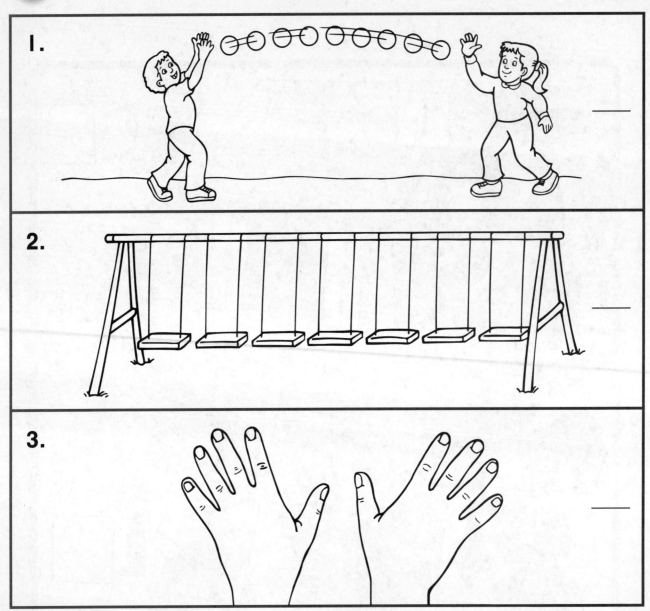

1. _____

2. _____

3. _____

5 **Trace. Write.**

10 10 ____ 10 ____

6 Listen and point. Cut and say. Glue on page 67. ✂

7 Glue. Play a game.

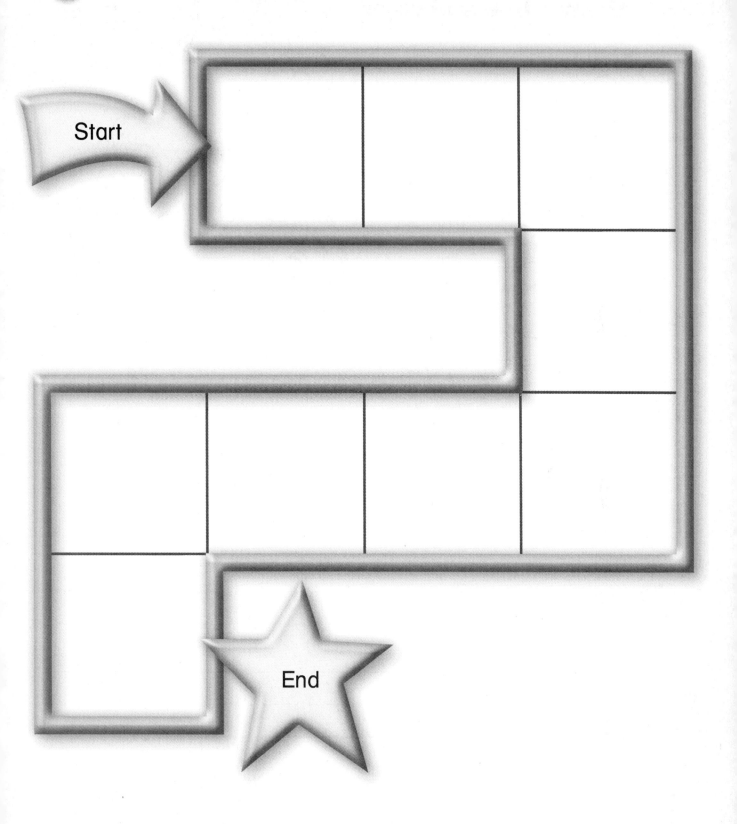

Start

End

Students glue the cards they cut out from page 65. In pairs or small groups, players move one space at a time. If they can name the picture they land on, they stay on that spot. If not, they go back one space.

8 **Listen and chant.**
   Draw a line and color.

U T S

S

t u

9 **Trace. Write.**

Ss   S   s

Tt   T   t

Uu   U   u

10 **Read *Having Fun!* Look and write.**

1

11 **Do you like the story? Draw a face.**

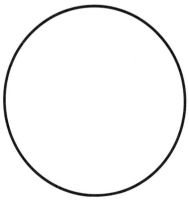

Review

12 **Listen and circle.**

1.

2.

3.

4.

5.
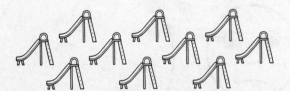 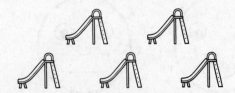

Animal Friends

1 Listen and color. Cut and glue. ✂

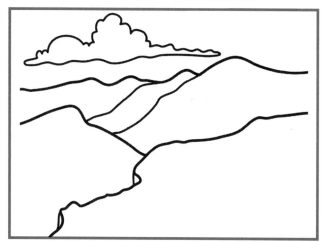

Students listen to the song and color the pictures. They cut out the animals and glue them in the appropriate places above.

Unit 8

71

2 **Help them out. Draw a path.**
What do you see? Listen and check.

3 **How many legs do you see? Write.**

_____

_____

_____

_____

Cut and say. Use on page 77. ✂️

5 Play a game. Match the cards. Say the name.

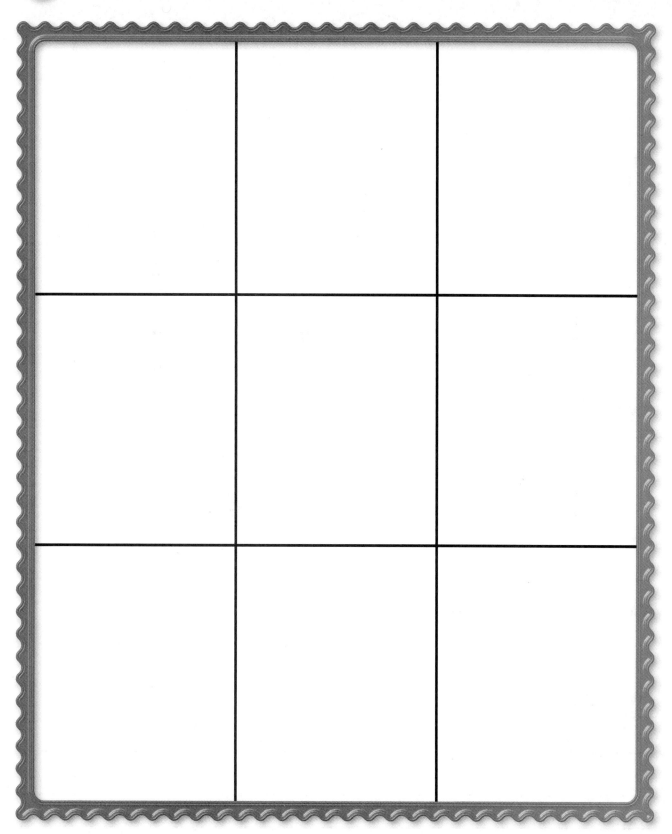

Students play with a partner. Each student places the cards he or she cut out from page 75
face down on his or her own page. Partners take turns uncovering one card from each page
to find a match. Then they name the cards they turn over.

6 Listen and chant. Draw a line.

V   W

W   x

X   v

7 Trace. Write.

V v   V   v

W w   W   w

X x   X   x

8 Listen to *Henrietta Hippo*. Draw a line.

1. Henrietta Hippo is moving to the zoo.

2. Henrietta is sad.

3. A bird is flying.

4. The animals are singing.

 Do you like the story? Draw a face.

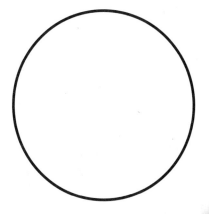

Unit 8

79

Review

10 Listen and circle.

1.

2.

3.

4.

5.

TRACK 42

1 Listen and sing. Cut and glue.

Students listen to and sing the song. They cut out the pictures and glue each in the appropriate place above.

2 Count. Write the number and say.

 _____

 _____

 _____

 _____

 _____

 _____

3 **Listen and point. Ask and answer.**

Cut and say. Glue on page 87.

TRACK 44

5 Listen. Ask and answer. Glue.

I like...   I don't like...

Play the audio or read the audioscript as a model. Students hold up a cutout and ask their partners *Do you like (apples)?* The partners answer and glue the cutout into the correct column, based on whether or not they like the food. Then students switch roles. Continue until all the cutouts are glued on the chart.

6 **Listen and chant.
Draw a line and color.**

TRACK 45

7 **Trace. Write.**

Y y   Y   y

Z z   Z   z

TRACK 46

8 Listen to *In the Park*. Draw a line.

9 Do you like the story? Draw a face.

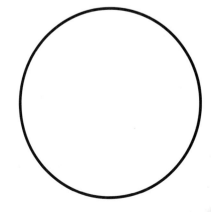

Review

10 Listen and circle.

1.

2.

3.

4.

5.

book

chair

circle

crayon

glue

one

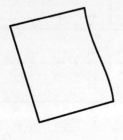
paper

pencil

scissors

teacher

three

two

bathroom

bedroom

brother

father

four

grandfather

grandmother

kitchen

living room

mother

sister

square

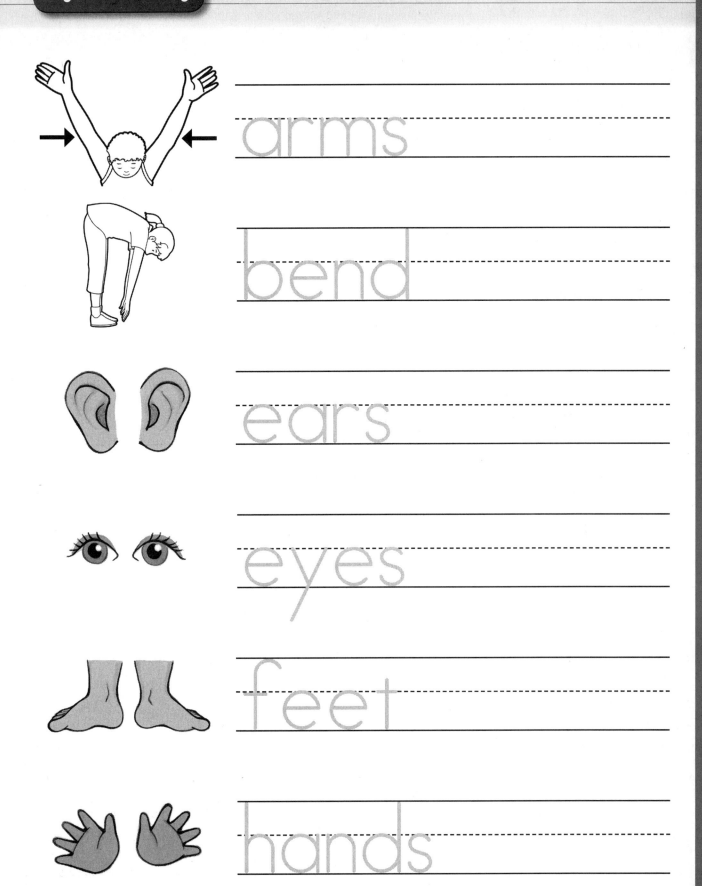

arms

bend

ears

eyes

feet

hands

 happy

 legs

 mouth

 nose

 sad

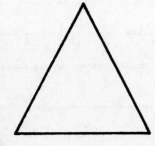 triangle

backpack

dress

five

hat

jacket

pants

rectangle

shirt

shoes

shorts

sweater

umbrella

airplane

ball

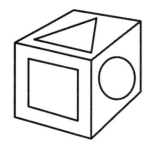

block

car

doll

game

robot

seven

six

teddy bear

train

truck

bus

dentist

doctor

eight

firefighter

fire truck

9 nine

 nurse

 police officer

 shopkeeper

 taxi

 toothbrush

climb

down

jump

jungle gym

kick

run

sing

slide

swing

ten

throw

up

bear

bird

cat

dog

elephant

fish

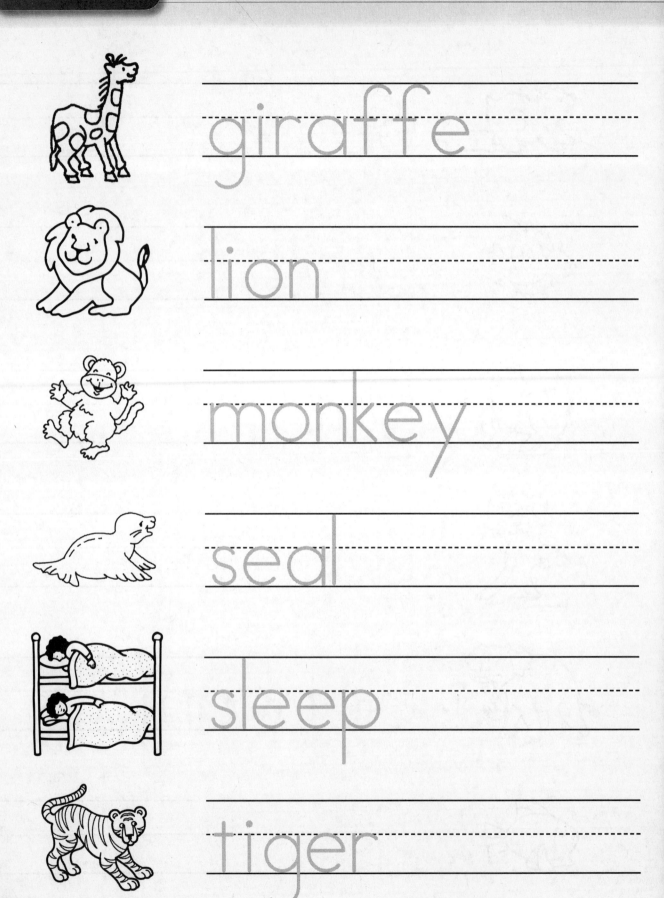

giraffe

lion

monkey

seal

sleep

tiger

 apple

 balloons

 banana

 bounce

 cake

 cookie

 ice cream

 lemonade

 orange

 sandwich

 sit

 tree